BACH MEETS JAZZ

15 WELL-TEMPERED CLASSICS ARRANGED BY PHILLIP KEVEREN

— PIANO LEVEL —
LATE INTERMEDIATE/EARLY ADVANCED

ISBN 978-1-4950-7664-0

HAL•LEONARD®
7777 W. BLUEMOUND RD. P.O. BOX 13819 MILWAUKEE, WI 53213

In Australia Contact:
Hal Leonard Australia Pty. Ltd.
4 Lentara Court
Cheltenham, Victoria, 3192 Australia
Email: ausadmin@halleonard.com.au

Visit Hal Leonard Online at
www.halleonard.com

Visit Phillip at
www.phillipkeveren.com

PREFACE

The harmonic language of jazz is built upon the rock of Bach. Johann Sebastian Bach. It's amazing to think that one musician – indeed, one who left us over 250 years ago – could have such a profound and sustaining impact on an art form. The "ii–V–I" chord progression, so integral to jazz, was perfected in the works of this great composer. These harmonies became the threads holding together the popular songs of George Gershwin, Irving Berlin, Jerome Kern, et al., which then became the platforms for jazz improvisation.

This collection of arrangements is my personal jazzy tribute to the Baroque master. Myriad recordings I have heard through the years that have explored this concept of "mashing up" jazz and Bach inspire these settings.

Musically yours,

Recordings to instruct and inspire…

The Swingle Singers	*Jazz Sebastian Bach* (1963)
Jacques Loussier	*Jacques Loussier Plays Bach* (No. 1 & 2) (2000)
The Classical Jazz Quartet	*Play Bach* (featuring Kenny Barron, et al.) (2006)

BIOGRAPHY

Phillip Keveren, a multi-talented keyboard artist and composer, has composed original works in a variety of genres from piano solo to symphonic orchestra. Mr. Keveren gives frequent concerts and workshops for teachers and their students in the United States, Canada, Europe, and Asia. Mr. Keveren holds a B.M. in composition from California State University Northridge and a M.M. in composition from the University of Southern California.

CONTENTS

JESU, JOY OF MAN'S DESIRING

BWV 147

By JOHANN SEBASTIAN BACH
Arranged by Phillip Keveren

21
D/C
Gmaj7
Am9
Gmaj9
Em11
Am7
D13
D7♭9
p
26
Gmaj7
Am7
Gmaj9
Cmaj9
D7sus
Em13
30
Cmaj9
B♭2
E♭maj7/B♭
B♭maj7
E♭2/G
Cm
B♭/D
E♭maj7
34
F
F7
B♭
B♭/A
E♭/G
B♭maj7/F
E♭maj9
Cm7♭5
mf
38
G2
G9
D9/G
Em7/G
D9
mp
molto rit.
42
Gmaj9
Am7
Gmaj7/B
Em7(4)
Am
G/B
Am/C
C♯m7♭5
D7sus
Gmaj9
A/G
a tempo
pp

JESUS, PRICELESS TREASURE

BWV 227

By JOHANN SEBASTIAN BACH
Arranged by Phillip Keveren

MARCH IN D MAJOR

BWV Anh. 122
from NOTEBOOK FOR ANNA MAGDALENA BACH

By C.P.E. BACH
Arranged by Phillip Keveren

18
A/E E7 A A13
sfz p
21
A E7 A E7 A N.C.
24
G E7 A F#7
cresc.
27
Bm Bm7 B♭7 A7 G
mf
30
A D A13 D7#9
f

33
G/D D N.C.
8va
p
36
G E7
cresc.
39
A F♯7 Bm Bm7 B♭7 A7
mf
42
G A D A13
f
45
D7♯9 G/D D E♭ D
p
f

LITTLE PRELUDE IN C MINOR

BWV 999

By JOHANN SEBASTIAN BACH
Arranged by Phillip Keveren

Gm/D
D7♭9
E♭maj7
D7♯5
C♯dim7/D
23
p
mp
Am7♭5/D
D7
Gm6
D7♭9
Gm/D
28
mf
Am7♭5/D
D7♭9
D7
Cdim7/G
G
F♯dim7/G
33
dim.
p
G
G7♭9
Cm/G
F♯dim7/G
38
rit.
G
Cm6/G
G
Gmaj9
43

LITTLE PRELUDE IN D MINOR

BWV 935

By JOHANN SEBASTIAN BACH
Arranged by Phillip Keveren

21
Fmaj7
Gm
B♭m/D♭
C7
G♭maj7
F6
25
F
C
Dm2
Gm/B♭
Adim7
p
mf
29
Gm7
Gm6
E♭maj7/G
D7♭9
Gm
Dsus/G
p
33
Gm2
Gm(add4)
Em7♭5
A
f
p
38
Dm
(Asus)
D
D(add4)
42
Dm/A
A7
Dm
Em7♭5
Dm/F
Gm9
A7♭9
Dm(maj7)
f
rit.

MENUET IN G MAJOR

BWV Anh. 114
from NOTEBOOK FOR ANNA MAGDALENA BACH

By CHRISTIAN PETZOLD
Arranged by Phillip Keveren

17
G2
Cmaj7
B7♯5
B♭13
21
Am7
Cm6/E♭
G/D
D7
G
25
Gmaj7
D9
Em9
A
p
29
D/A
A
D/A
A7
D7
33
G
Cmaj7
D13
Cmaj7(add6)
F6/9(♯11)
A13
D7♯9
f

37
D7
G/D
D
G
D9
G6
mf
41
C
F13
C6/9
45
F6/9
Cmaj7(add6)
D13♯11
G9
p cresc.
49
C
F13
C6/9
f
53
Fm
C6/9
G7
C
C9♯11
p cresc.
f

MENUET IN G MINOR

BWV Anh. 115
from NOTEBOOK FOR ANNA MAGDALENA BACH

By CHRISTIAN PETZOLD
Arranged by Phillip Keveren

D7♯5(♯9)
Bdim7
Cm/B♭
F7♭9
E♭maj9
F7♭9
20
p
24
B♭6
B♭7♭5
F6/9
Gm7♭5
mp
Fmaj7
F7
A♭/G♭
G/F
F/E♭
B♭sus2/D
28
p
mf
Gm7♭5/D♭
G/B
Cm
Gm/B♭
D7♭9/A
Gm6
32
D7♯5(♯9)
E♭13♯11
E♭maj9
D
36
p

C2
D7♭9
Gm2
Dm/F
40
mf
E♭maj7
D7♯5(♯9)
E♭2/G
B♭maj7/F
44
p
E♭maj7
D7sus
D7
Gm2
Dm6
48
mp
E♭maj7
D7
Bdim7
Cm2
52
mf
E♭maj7
F13
N.C.
B♭2
56
p

MUSETTE IN D MAJOR

BWV Anh. 126

from NOTEBOOK FOR ANNA MAGDALENA BACH

Composer unknown
Arranged by Phillip Keveren

16
Bm7
E
N.C.
19
22
Bm7
B♭7♭5
A7
D
25
D♭6/9(♯11)
F13♭9
A7
D
28
C7
B7
B♭7♭5
A13
Dadd9
8vb

PRELUDE AND FUGUE IN C MINOR

BWV 847

from THE WELL-TEMPERED CLAVIER, BOOK 1

By JOHANN SEBASTIAN BACH
Arranged by Phillip Keveren

12
B♭(4)
f
E♭2
rit.
14
Cm
p cresc.
a tempo
Dm7♭5/C
16
E♭/B♭
F7
18
B♭7♭9
mf
G7♭9
20
Cm
f
Dm7♭5/C
22
F♯dim/C
Cm/G

24
F♯dim7/G
E♭maj7/G
26
Dm7♭5/G
rit.
G7♭9
♩ = 60
28
Cm
Dm7♭5/C
Cm
Dm7♭5/C
N.C.
mf
31
33
35
rit.
(Cm)
p
(Cm9)

PRELUDE IN C MAJOR

BWV 846
from THE WELL-TEMPERED CLAVIER, BOOK 1

By JOHANN SEBASTIAN BACH
Arranged by Phillip Keveren

G2
Gdim7
11
Dm7/F
Fdim7
13
p
C2/E
Cmaj7/E
Fmaj7/E
15
cresc.
Dm7
G9
17
8
f
dim. e rit.
5 2 1 3
3
G7♭9/C
C2
C9
19
pp
mp
5 2 1 4 3
21
Fmaj7
F♯dim7
1 2

A♭dim7
23
poco rit.
G9
p cresc. poco a poco
a tempo
C/G
25
F/G
C2
C
Cmaj7
C6
G9
27
f
mp cresc.
F♯dim7/G
29
C/G
G7sus
31
p
rit.
C7
mp
Fmaj7/C
34
G7/C
C
molto rit.

SHEEP MAY SAFELY GRAZE

BWV 208

By JOHANN SEBASTIAN BACH
Arranged by Phillip Keveren

Cm7
B♭maj7 F9 Gm7 E♭m6/G♭
F
E♭/F
E9♯11 E♭9 D9 D♭9♯11
13
rit. e dim.
mp a tempo
A♭maj7/C F♯dim7 Gm6
Cm2
Cm/B♭
A♭maj7
Cm/G
16
cresc.
Fm9
G/F
Cm7(4)
G7♭9
Cm2
A♭maj7
19
f
p
G7♭9
A♭maj7
22
mf
Fm9
G7 A♭maj7
Cm/G G7
C
B♭13 G7sus(♯9)
24
f
rit.
mf a tempo

Dm2
E♭6/9(♯11)
Fmaj7
Bm7
Em7
26
A9
Cm6/D
G
G7♯5
Cmaj9
Am9
28
mp
Dm9
G13
C
Cmaj7
Fmaj7/A
C2/G
30
Fmaj7
C2/E
Dm7
G7sus
C2
Fmaj7/C
32
Bdim7/C
C2
34
rit.

SLEEPERS, AWAKE

BWV 140

By JOHANN SEBASTIAN BACH
Arranged by Phillip Keveren

15
B♭2/D E♭maj7 E♭2/G B♭maj7/F F9 B♭ E♭2 A♭maj7/C
18
A♭maj7 E♭2 A♭maj7/C A♭maj7
mf
21
E♭2 A♭maj7/C E♭2
p
mf
24
A♭maj7/C A2 F♯m2 D2
p
mf
27
A2 F♯m2 D2 E/A A C♯m7 Bm7 E7 D9
p

30
A2/C♯ Bm7 E7 A2 F♯m2 B7
mp
33
E Emaj7 A/C♯ E/B F♯m/A Amaj7/G♯ B9/F♯ Esus
f
mf
35
E2/G♯ Amaj7 A2/C♯ Emaj7/B B9 E A2/E
p
38
E7sus A2 D2/F♯ D2
mf
41
E/A A D2/F♯ A
p
rit.

TOCCATA AND FUGUE IN D MINOR

BWV 565

By JOHANN SEBASTIAN BACH
Arranged by Phillip Keveren

21
Edim7
Dm6
C13
24
C9
Fmaj7/C
C7♭9
27
B♭m6(maj7)
A7
A7♭9
A7♭9/D
p
f
30
N.C.
freely
tr
Dm
p
33
Dm2/A
A7♭9
Dm6/A
a tempo
36
A7♭9
Dm/A
A7♭9
Dm/A
A7
cresc. poco a poco

39
Dm/A
A7
Dm/A
A
Dm
f
42
46
A7
Dm
p
50
54
A/G
Dm/F
Gm/B♭
A7
Dsus
Dm
ff
molto rit.
60
Swing (♩ = 168)
N.C.
mf
1

64
68
Gm2
Cm7
F7♭9
B♭maj7
Em7♭5
A7
71
N.C.
75
79
B♭/D
Am/C
f
83
Gm/B♭
A7♭9
B♭maj7/D
Am7/C
B♭6
A7♭5
B♭13
A7♯5
p
mf
rit.

Brightly (♩ = 208)
87
Dm
p cresc.
91
f
95
A7
Dm
p
99
102
A7♭9
ff
105
Dm

TWO-PART INVENTION IN A MINOR

BWV 784

By JOHANN SEBASTIAN BACH
Arranged by Phillip Keveren

17
Cmaj7/G
Fm6/G
C6/G
G13♭9
C6/G
G7
p
20
C2/G
G7♯5
Am9
D9/A
mf
23
Gmaj9
Cmaj7/G
B9
p
26
Cmaj7/E
D9
B♭7♭5
E♭9
mf
29
F♯m7♭5
B7♭9
Em9
p rit.
32
A7♭9/E
A7♭9/C♯
Dm6
a tempo
mf

35
G7♭9/B
C2
C6
F♯dim7
38
E7♭9
Am2
mf
41
F2
E7♭9
Am2
Fmaj7
44
Am7
Dm7
G9
47
C2
Fmaj7
F6
Em7
C/E
50
Dm7
E7
Am2
Fmaj7
Am9(maj7)
rit.
p
pp

TWO-PART INVENTION IN F MAJOR

BWV 779

By JOHANN SEBASTIAN BACH
Arranged by Phillip Keveren

17
E♭2 Cm9 A7♭9 Dm(maj7) Dm7
f
21
Gm9/C C9 Fmaj7/A G7♭5 G7 Fmaj7 Fmaj7♭5 Fmaj7♯5
p
24
B♭maj7/D Fmaj7/C F7/C B♭maj7
f
27
Gm9 E♭maj7 C2 C7
30
F2 F7 B♭
4
2 1
32
4
Dm7 Gm7 C E♭2 F

THE PHILLIP KEVEREN SERIES

PIANO SOLO

00156644 **ABBA for Classical Piano** $15.99
00311024 **Above All** $12.99
00311348 **Americana** $12.99
00198473 **Bach Meets Jazz** $14.99
00313594 **Bacharach and David** $15.99
00306412 **The Beatles** $19.99
00312189 **The Beatles for Classical Piano** $17.99
00275876 **The Beatles – Recital Suites** $19.99
00312546 **Best Piano Solos** $15.99
00156601 **Blessings** $14.99
00198656 **Blues Classics** $14.99
00284359 **Broadway Songs with a Classical Flair** $14.99
00310669 **Broadway's Best** $16.99
00312106 **Canzone Italiana** $12.99
00280848 **Carpenters** $17.99
00310629 **A Celtic Christmas** $14.99
00310549 **The Celtic Collection** $14.99
00280571 **Celtic Songs with a Classical Flair** $12.99
00263362 **Charlie Brown Favorites** $14.99
00312190 **Christmas at the Movies** $15.99
00294754 **Christmas Carols with a Classical Flair** $12.99
00311414 **Christmas Medleys** $14.99
00236669 **Christmas Praise Hymns** $12.99
00233788 **Christmas Songs for Classical Piano** $14.99
00311769 **Christmas Worship Medleys** $14.99
00310607 **Cinema Classics** $15.99
00301857 **Circles** $10.99
00311101 **Classic Wedding Songs** $12.99
00311292 **Classical Folk** $10.95
00311083 **Classical Jazz** $14.99
00137779 **Coldplay for Classical Piano** $16.99
00311103 **Contemporary Wedding Songs** $12.99
00348788 **Country Songs with a Classical Flair** $14.99
00249097 **Disney Recital Suites** $17.99
00311754 **Disney Songs for Classical Piano** $17.99
00241379 **Disney Songs for Ragtime Piano** $17.99
00364812 **The Essential Hymn Anthology** $34.99
00311881 **Favorite Wedding Songs** $14.99
00315974 **Fiddlin' at the Piano** $12.99
00311811 **The Film Score Collection** $15.99
00269408 **Folksongs with a Classical Flair** $12.99
00144353 **The Gershwin Collection** $14.99
00233789 **Golden Scores** $14.99
00144351 **Gospel Greats** $14.99
00183566 **The Great American Songbook** $14.99
00312084 **The Great Melodies** $14.99
00311157 **Great Standards** $14.99
00171621 **A Grown-Up Christmas List** $14.99
00311071 **The Hymn Collection** $14.99
00311349 **Hymn Medleys** $14.99
00280705 **Hymns in a Celtic Style** $14.99
00269407 **Hymns with a Classical Flair** $14.99
00311249 **Hymns with a Touch of Jazz** $14.99
00310905 **I Could Sing of Your Love Forever** $16.99
00310762 **Jingle Jazz** $15.99
00175310 **Billy Joel for Classical Piano** $16.99
00126449 **Elton John for Classical Piano** $19.99
00310839 **Let Freedom Ring!** $12.99
00238988 **Andrew Lloyd Webber Piano Songbook** $14.99
00313227 **Andrew Lloyd Webber Solos** $17.99
00313523 **Mancini Magic** $16.99
00312113 **More Disney Songs for Classical Piano** $16.99
00311295 **Motown Hits** $14.99
00300640 **Piano Calm** $12.99
00339131 **Piano Calm: Christmas** $14.99
00346009 **Piano Calm: Prayer** $14.99
00306870 **Piazzolla Tangos** $17.99
00386709 **Praise and Worship for Classical Piano** $14.99
00156645 **Queen for Classical Piano** $17.99
00310755 **Richard Rodgers Classics** $17.99
00289545 **Scottish Songs** $12.99
00119403 **The Sound of Music** $16.99
00311978 **The Spirituals Collection** $12.99
00366023 **So Far...** $14.99
00210445 **Star Wars** $16.99
00224738 **Symphonic Hymns for Piano** $14.99
00366022 **Three-Minute Encores** $16.99
00279673 **Tin Pan Alley** $12.99
00312112 **Treasured Hymns for Classical Piano** $15.99
00144926 **The Twelve Keys of Christmas** $14.99
00278486 **The Who for Classical Piano** $16.99
00294036 **Worship with a Touch of Jazz** $14.99
00311911 **Yuletide Jazz** $19.99

EASY PIANO

00210401 **Adele for Easy Classical Piano** $17.99
00310610 **African-American Spirituals** $12.99
00218244 **The Beatles for Easy Classical Piano** $14.99
00218387 **Catchy Songs for Piano** $12.99
00310973 **Celtic Dreams** $12.99
00233686 **Christmas Carols for Easy Classical Piano** $14.99
00311126 **Christmas Pops** $16.99
00368199 **Christmas Reflections** $14.99
00311548 **Classic Pop/Rock Hits** $14.99
00310769 **A Classical Christmas** $14.99
00310975 **Classical Movie Themes** $12.99
00144352 **Disney Songs for Easy Classical Piano** $14.99
00311093 **Early Rock 'n' Roll** $14.99
00311997 **Easy Worship Medleys** $14.99
00289547 **Duke Ellington** $14.99
00160297 **Folksongs for Easy Classical Piano** $12.99
00110374 **George Gershwin Classics** $14.99
00310805 **Gospel Treasures** $14.99
00306821 **Vince Guaraldi Collection** $19.99
00160294 **Hymns for Easy Classical Piano** $14.99
00310798 **Immortal Hymns** $12.99
00311294 **Jazz Standards** $12.99
00355474 **Living Hope** $14.99
00310744 **Love Songs** $14.99
00233740 **The Most Beautiful Songs for Easy Classical Piano** $12.99
00220036 **Pop Ballads** $14.99
00311406 **Pop Gems of the 1950s** $12.95
00233739 **Pop Standards for Easy Classical Piano** $12.99
00102887 **A Ragtime Christmas** $12.99
00311293 **Ragtime Classics** $14.99
00312028 **Santa Swings** $14.99
00233688 **Songs from Childhood for Easy Classical Piano** $12.99
00103258 **Songs of Inspiration** $14.99
00310840 **Sweet Land of Liberty** $12.99
00126450 **10,000 Reasons** $16.99
00310712 **Timeless Praise** $14.99
00311086 **TV Themes** $14.99
00310717 **21 Great Classics** $14.99
00160076 **Waltzes & Polkas for Easy Classical Piano** $12.99
00145342 **Weekly Worship** $17.99

BIG-NOTE PIANO

00310838 **Children's Favorite Movie Songs** $14.99
00346000 **Christmas Movie Magic** $12.99
00277368 **Classical Favorites** $12.99
00277370 **Disney Favorites** $14.99
00310888 **Joy to the World** $12.99
00310908 **The Nutcracker** $12.99
00277371 **Star Wars** $16.99

BEGINNING PIANO SOLOS

00311202 **Awesome God** $14.99
00310837 **Christian Children's Favorites** $14.99
00311117 **Christmas Traditions** $10.99
00311250 **Easy Hymns** $12.99
00102710 **Everlasting God** $10.99
00311403 **Jazzy Tunes** $10.95
00310822 **Kids' Favorites** $12.99
00367778 **A Magical Christmas** $14.99
00338175 **Silly Songs for Kids** $9.99

PIANO DUET

00126452 **The Christmas Variations** $14.99
00362562 **Classic Piano Duets** $14.99
00311350 **Classical Theme Duets** $12.99
00295099 **Gospel Duets** $12.99
00311544 **Hymn Duets** $14.99
00311203 **Praise & Worship Duets** $14.99
00294755 **Sacred Christmas Duets** $14.99
00119405 **Star Wars** $16.99
00253545 **Worship Songs for Two** $12.99

Prices, contents, and availability subject to change without notice.

jazz piano solos series

INCLUDES CHORD NAMES!

Each volume features exciting new arrangements with chord symbols of the songs which helped define a style.

vol. 1 miles davis
00306521 .... $19.99

vol. 2 jazz blues
00306522 .... $17.99

vol. 3 latin jazz
00310621 .... $16.99

vol. 4 bebop jazz
00310709 .... $16.99

vol. 5 cool jazz
00310710 .... $16.99

vol. 6 hard bop
00323507 .... $16.99

vol. 7 smooth jazz
00310727 .... $16.99

vol. 8 jazz pop
00311786 .... $17.99

vol. 9 duke ellington
00311787 .... $17.99

vol. 10 jazz ballads
00311788 .... $17.99

vol. 11 soul jazz
00311789 .... $17.99

vol. 12 swinging jazz
00311797 .... $17.99

vol. 13 jazz gems
00311899 .... $16.99

vol. 14 jazz classics
00311900 .... $16.99

vol. 15 bossa nova
00311906 .... $17.99

vol. 16 disney
00312121 .... $17.99

vol. 17 antonio carlos jobim
00312122 .... $17.99

vol. 18 modern jazz quartet
00307270 .... $16.99

vol. 19 bill evans
00307273 .... $19.99

vol. 20 gypsy jazz
00307289 .... $16.99

vol. 21 new orleans
00312169 .... $16.99

vol. 22 classic jazz
00001529 .... $17.99

vol. 23 jazz for lovers
00312548 .... $16.99

vol. 24 john coltrane
00307395 .... $17.99

vol. 25 christmas songs
00101790 .... $17.99

vol. 26 george gershwin
00103353 .... $17.99

vol. 27 late night jazz
00312547 .... $17.99

vol. 28 the beatles
00119302 .... $19.99

vol. 29 elton john
00120968 .... $19.99

vol. 30 cole porter
00123364 .... $17.99

vol. 31 cocktail piano
00123366 .... $17.99

vol. 32 johnny mercer
00123367 .... $16.99

vol. 33 gospel
00127079 .... $17.99

vol. 34 horace silver
00139633 .... $16.99

vol. 35 stride piano
00139685 .... $17.99

vol. 36 broadway jazz
00144365 .... $17.99

vol. 37 silver screen jazz
00144366 .... $16.99

vol. 38 henry mancini
00146382 .... $16.99

vol. 39 sacred christmas carols
00147678 .... $17.99

vol. 40 charlie parker
00149089 .... $16.99

vol. 41 pop standards
00153656 .... $16.99

vol. 42 dave brubeck
00154634 .... $16.99

vol. 43 candlelight jazz
00154901 .... $17.99

vol. 44 jazz standards
00160856 .... $17.99

vol. 45 christmas standards
00172024 .... $17.99

vol. 46 cocktail jazz
00172025 .... $17.99

vol. 47 hymns
00172026 .... $17.99

vol. 48 blue skies & other irving berlin songs
00197873 .... $16.99

vol. 49 thelonious monk
00232767 .... $16.99

vol. 50 best smooth jazz
00233277 .... $16.99

vol. 51 disney favorites
00233315 .... $16.99

vol. 52 bebop classics
00234075 .... $16.99

vol. 53 jazz-rock
00256715 .... $16.99

vol. 54 jazz fusion
00256716 .... $16.99

vol. 55 ragtime
00274961 .... $16.99

vol. 56 pop ballads
00274962 .... $16.99

vol. 57 pat metheny
00277058 .... $17.99

vol. 58 big band era
00284837 .... $17.99

vol. 59 west coast jazz
00290792 .... $17.99

vol. 60 boogie woogie
00363280 .... $17.99

vol. 61 christmas classics
00367872 .... $17.99

HAL•LEONARD®

View songlists and order online from your favorite music retailer at
www.halleonard.com

0621

Prices, contents & availability subject to change without notice.

ALL JAZZED UP!

FROM HAL LEONARD

In this series, popular favorites receive unexpected fresh treatments. Uniquely reimagined and crafted for intermediate piano solo, these tunes have been All Jazzed Up!

J.S. BACH
Air on the G String • Aria • Bist du bei mir (Be Thou with Me) • Gavotte • Jesu, Joy of Man's Desiring • Largo • March • Minuet in G • Musette • Sheep May Safely Graze • Siciliano • Sleepers, Awake (Wachet Auf).
00151064........$12.99

THE BEATLES
All My Loving • And I Love Her • Come Together • Eight Days a Week • Eleanor Rigby • The Fool on the Hill • Here, There and Everywhere • Lady Madonna • Lucy in the Sky with Diamonds • Michelle • While My Guitar Gently Weeps • Yesterday.
00172235........$12.99

CHRISTMAS CAROLS
Auld Lang Syne • Deck the Hall • The First Noel • Good King Wenceslas • In the Bleak Midwinter • Jingle Bells • Joy to the World • O Christmas Tree • O Come, All Ye Faithful • O Little Town of Bethlehem • Up on the Housetop • We Wish You a Merry Christmas.
00277866........$12.99

CHRISTMAS SONGS
Blue Christmas • The Christmas Song (Chestnuts Roasting on an Open Fire) • Christmas Time Is Here • Do You Hear What I Hear • Feliz Navidad • Have Yourself a Merry Little Christmas • I'll Be Home for Christmas • Merry Christmas, Darling • Silver Bells • Sleigh Ride • White Christmas • Winter Wonderland.
00236706........$12.99

COLDPLAY
Clocks • Don't Panic • Every Teardrop Is a Waterfall • Fix You • Magic • Paradise • The Scientist • A Sky Full of Stars • Speed of Sound • Trouble • Viva La Vida • Yellow.
00149026........$12.99

DISNEY
Belle • Circle of Life • Cruella De Vil • Ev'rybody Wants to Be a Cat • It's a Small World • Let It Go • Mickey Mouse March • Once upon a Dream • Part of Your World • Supercalifragilisticexpialidocious • Under the Sea • When She Loved Me.
00151072........$14.99

JIMI HENDRIX
Castles Made of Sand • Crosstown Traffic • Fire • Foxey Lady • Hey Joe • Little Wing • Manic Depression • Purple Haze • Spanish Castle Magic • The Wind Cries Mary.
00174441........$12.99

BILLY JOEL
And So It Goes • Honesty • It's Still Rock and Roll to Me • Just the Way You Are • The Longest Time • Lullabye (Goodnight, My Angel) • My Life • New York State of Mind • Piano Man • The River of Dreams • She's Always a Woman • She's Got a Way.
00149039........$12.99

MOTOWN
Ain't Nothing like the Real Thing • How Sweet It Is (To Be Loved by You) • I Can't Help Myself (Sugar Pie, Honey Bunch) • I Heard It Through the Grapevine • I Want You Back • Let's Get It On • My Girl • Never Can Say Goodbye • Overjoyed • Papa Was a Rollin' Stone • Still • You Can't Hurry Love.
00174482........$12.99

NIRVANA
About a Girl • All Apologies • Come as You Are • Dumb • Heart Shaped Box • In Bloom • Lithium • The Man Who Sold the World • On a Plain • (New Wave) Polly • Rape Me • Smells like Teen Spirit.
00149025........$12.99

OZZY OSBOURNE
Crazy Train • Dreamer • Flying High Again • Goodbye to Romance • Iron Man • Mama, I'm Coming Home • Mr. Crowley • No More Tears • Over the Mountain • Paranoid • Perry Mason • Time After Time.
00149040........$12.99

ELVIS PRESLEY
Blue Suede Shoes • Can't Help Falling in Love • Cryin' in the Chapel • Don't • Don't Be Cruel (To a Heart That's True) • Heartbreak Hotel • I Want You, I Need You, I Love You • Jailhouse Rock • Love Me Tender • Suspicious Minds • The Wonder of You • You Don't Have to Say You Love Me.
00198895........$12.99

STEVIE WONDER
As • Ebony and Ivory • For Once in My Life • I Just Called to Say I Love You • I Wish • Isn't She Lovely • My Cherie Amour • Ribbon in the Sky • Signed, Sealed, Delivered I'm Yours • Sir Duke • Superstition • You Are the Sunshine of My Life.
00149090........$12.99

HAL•LEONARD®
www.halleonard.com

Prices, contents and availability subject to change without notice.